I CAN BE...
BOLD

STRONG KINGS AND QUEENS WHO WERE GREAT LEADERS

BY SHALINI VALLEPUR

BookLife PUBLISHING

BookLife Publishing Ltd.
King's Lynn
Norfolk PE30 4LS

Printed in Malaysia.

A catalogue record for this book is available from the British Library.

ISBN: 978-1-78637-841-5

Written by:
Shalini Vallepur

Edited by:
Madeline Tyler

Designed by:
Danielle Jones

IMAGE CREDITS

All images are courtesy of Shutterstock.com, unless otherwise specified. With thanks to Getty Images, Thinkstock Photo and iStockphoto. Cover and throughout – asantosg, Forest Foxy, WINS86. 3 – CCat82. 6 – Lexver. 7 – Bist, Kram78. 8 – tramway5, BelayaMedvedica. 9 – Lars Poyansky. 10 – TizGroup, yui, Ernst Wallis et al [Public domain], babayuka. 11 – La Suerte Arte. 12 – primiaou, Vector Tradition. 13 – sebos. 14 – Vector Tradition, ArtMari. 15 – sculpies, Nagib. 16 – MrVayn, ArtMari, netsign33. 17 – Black creator, Jackan, ATeam. 18 – Morphart Creation, Beth Wizard, hchjjl. 19 – ADSKrongsawat, Irina Alexandrovna, vlastas. 20 – Maxger, Rorius. 21 – Alexander Smulskiy. 22 – antonpix. 23 – antonpix, Dorottya Mathe. 24–25 – RedlineVector, Dzm1try. 26 – Macrovector. 27 – TeddyandMia. 29 – rob zs.

CONTENTS

WORDS THAT LOOK LIKE this ARE EXPLAINED IN THE GLOSSARY ON PAGE 31.

I CAN BE...

BOLD

There have been many great leaders in the past. Kings, queens, princes and princesses have led people to find food, fight wars and build big cities. But what makes a good leader?

What does it mean to be bold? Maybe it is standing out from the crowd, or taking a big risk to do something that you think is right. Maybe being bold is being scared of something but doing it anyway to help other people.

We may not be leaders of a big **tribe** or a country of people, but we are the leaders of our own lives. What lessons can be learnt from the bold kings, queens, princes and princesses of the past? How can we be bold in our everyday lives?

HATSHEPSUT

Born: Around 1507 BC Died: Around 1458 BC

Hatshepsut was the daughter of Thutmose I, the **pharaoh** of Egypt. Hatshepsut was married to her half-brother. Marrying a family member was common in ancient Egypt at the time. When a pharaoh died, their son became the next leader. After Hatshepsut's father died, her half-brother, Thutmose II, became pharaoh. When Thutmose II died, his son, Thutmose III, became pharaoh.

Thutmose III was still very young, so Hatshepsut had the important job of acting as **regent** for her stepson. She became involved with the **government** in ancient Egypt and had many supporters. Hatshepsut decided to take control of ancient Egypt and, after seven years as regent, she was crowned pharaoh.

In order to fit the role of pharaoh and win people over, Hatshepsut wore the clothes that male pharaohs wore – she even wore a fake beard! During her 20-year rule, ancient Egypt was a peaceful place. Instead of going to war with other people like the pharaohs of the past did, Hatshepsut set up **trade** with them. Ancient Egypt became richer under her rule and Hatshepsut built many public buildings and statues of herself as pharaoh.

Today, we remember Hatshepsut as one of the most successful pharaohs of ancient Egypt.

"MY MOUTH IS EFFECTIVE IN ITS SPEECH;
I DO NOT GO BACK ON MY WORD."
- HATSHEPSUT

BE LIKE HATSHEPSUT

EGYPTIAN HIEROGLYPHS

Ancient Egyptians, including Hatshepsut, used pictures called hieroglyphs to write with. Each hieroglyph represented a sound, but some represented a full word or even a thought or feeling. Let's have a go at using hieroglyphs!

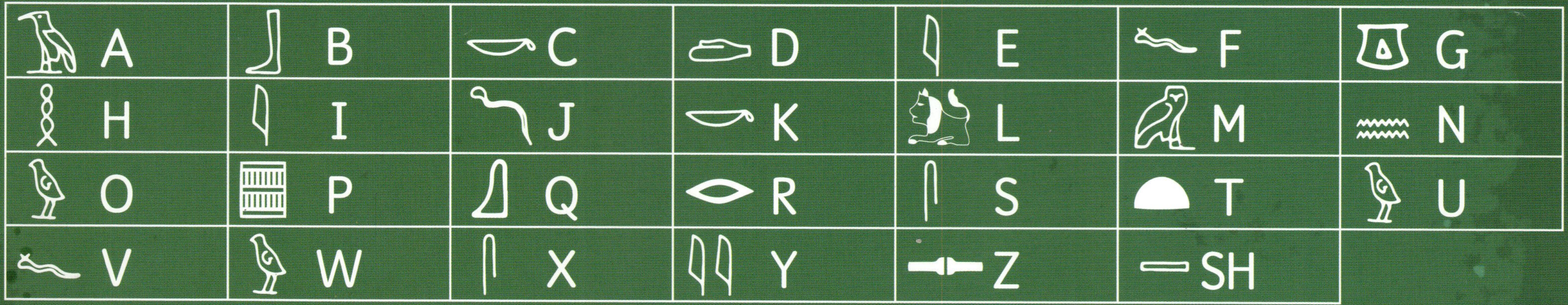

WHAT DOES IT SAY?

Grab a pencil and some paper and use the table to find out what has been written in hieroglyphs.

Try and make your own secret message using hieroglyphs for a friend or family member to translate.

Remember that the same hieroglyph can represent more than one sound!

If you could come up with your own hieroglyphs, what would they look like? Try and draw your own hieroglyphs for the following things:

- Dog
- Lunchtime
- Happy
- House

CYRUS THE GREAT

Born: Around 590 BC Died: 529 BC

Cyrus became the king of **Persia** when he was around 21 years old. He founded the **First Persian Empire** and set out to expand it into new lands. The only way to do this was to battle other groups of people and defeat them.

Cyrus was a great leader in battle, and he **conquered** many places. He wanted people to support him so he allowed them to follow their own religions and **cultures**, as long as they supported his rule. During this time, it was normal for leaders to treat people in conquered places very badly. Cyrus wanted to change this and make sure that people were happy to follow him. It didn't matter what religion or background somebody had, Cyrus treated everybody the same.

Cyrus's way of ruling was different to other leaders. He tried his best to improve the lives of his people. He helped to rebuild damaged temples and helped people to return to their homes when they were sent away for a long time. Cyrus the Great is remembered for his bold and kind leadership.

BE LIKE CYRUS
AND TREAT EVERYBODY FAIRLY.

"FREEDOM, DIGNITY, WEALTH –
THESE THREE TOGETHER CONSTITUTE
THE GREATEST HAPPINESS OF HUMANITY."
– CYRUS THE GREAT

ASHOKA THE GREAT

Born: 304 BC Died: 232 BC

Ashoka became the **emperor** of the **Mauryan Empire** in India. His father and grandfather ruled the empire before him and Ashoka followed them. Ashoka was a skilled fighter and he focused on making the Mauryan Empire bigger by conquering new lands with a huge army. Many people were killed during the battles and Ashoka himself was injured. Then Ashoka met some **monks** who taught him about **Buddhism**.

After learning about Buddhism from the monks, Ashoka made a huge change and began to practise Buddhist **dharma**. He saw the destruction that his conquests brought to people and realised that fighting wasn't the best way to lead an empire. Instead of conquering people through war, Ashoka began to spread Buddhism across his empire. He followed the Buddhist teachings that taught people to be honest, kind and good to everybody. Following this, Ashoka built hospitals and wells for people and animals. He taught people to be kind to animals and wanted everybody to live free and happy lives, whatever religion they followed.

Ashoka built great pillars and wrote his messages of the Buddhist dharma on them. Some of the pillars still stand today and remind us of how Ashoka made a bold change towards peace for all people.

"AND WHAT IS DHARMA? IT IS HAVING FEW FAULTS AND MANY GOOD DEEDS, MERCY, CHARITY, TRUTHFULNESS, AND PURITY."

– ASHOKA THE GREAT

CLEOPATRA

Born: Around 70–69 BC Died: 30 BC

Cleopatra was the daughter of the pharaoh Ptolemy XII and his wife Cleopatra V. Her father died when she was 18 years old and Cleopatra had to rule Egypt with her ten-year-old brother. Although her brother was pharaoh, Cleopatra was better at ruling Egypt. Her brother didn't like this, and forced Cleopatra to leave so that he could rule alone.

The Roman leader, Julius Caesar, came to Egypt. Cleopatra needed his help so that she could become pharaoh. Together, they defeated her brother and Cleopatra became pharaoh. Cleopatra was a clever and bold pharaoh. She managed to **unite** people who were fighting. Cleopatra loved Egypt and did her best to keep Egyptian culture strong.

When Caesar was killed, Mark Antony became leader of Rome. Cleopatra fell in love with Mark Antony and together they ruled Egypt. They were popular rulers and together they spread Egyptian rule to new lands. This was important as there were not many female rulers who were as loved and famous as Cleopatra. Both Cleopatra and Mark Antony died when they tried to take control of Rome.

"I WILL NOT BE TRIUMPHED OVER."
- CLEOPATRA
BE LIKE CLEOPATRA
AND LOVE WHERE YOU LIVE.

BOUDICCA

Born: Around AD 25–30 Died: Around AD 61–62

Boudicca was born in England and was part of a **Celtic** tribe called the Iceni. Boudicca married the leader of the Iceni, King Prasutagus, and became the Queen of the Iceni. During this time, the **Roman Empire** ruled parts of England, but the Romans let King Prasutagus lead the Iceni, as long as they followed strict Roman rules.

When King Prasutagus died, he left half of the Iceni land with Boudicca and her daughters and the other half with the Roman Empire. He thought that doing this would keep the Iceni people safe. But the Romans wanted the land for themselves. They attacked Boudicca and her daughters in the streets to show all the Iceni that the lands belonged to the Romans. The rest of the Iceni tribe were angry at the Romans for treating their queen so badly.

Boudicca decided to start a **rebellion** against the Romans. Other tribes joined her and the Iceni to fight back against the harsh Roman rule. Under Boudicca's brave leadership, the tribes destroyed three Roman cities, including Londinium, which we now call London.

The Romans began to fight back against Boudicca and the tribes. The tribes fought bravely, but they were overwhelmed by the Romans. Boudicca didn't want to be taken prisoner. It is believed that she drank poison to escape Roman capture. Boudicca is remembered for her bravery.

"I AM FIGHTING AS AN ORDINARY PERSON FOR MY LOST FREEDOM, MY BRUISED BODY, AND MY OUTRAGED DAUGHTERS."

– BOUDICCA

BE LIKE BOUDICCA AND STAND UP FOR YOURSELF WHEN YOU NEED TO.

ALFRED THE GREAT

Born: 849 Died: 899

Alfred was born in Wessex, a kingdom in what is now England. His father, Aethewulf, was the king of Wessex. England was made up of different kingdoms during this time, and they all faced a big threat. A group of Vikings, called the Danes, had landed in England to steal the riches of the different kingdoms.

When the Danes reached Wessex, Alfred helped to lead the army of Wessex against the Danes. When his father and his four elder brothers died, Alfred became king and it was his job to protect Wessex.

King Alfred realised that making peace with the Danes was better than fighting them. He made a bold move and gave the Danes their own land, which was called Danelaw. When the fighting stopped, King Alfred focused on making life better for his people. He set up schools and he translated books from Latin into Old English, so that everybody could understand them. King Alfred also set up laws. These laws were fair, and helped to protect everybody living in his kingdom.

BE LIKE ALFRED AND FIND
A PEACEFUL WAY TO SOLVE PROBLEMS.

"I DESIRE TO LEAVE TO THE PEOPLE THAT
COME AFTER ME A REMEMBRANCE OF ME
IN GOOD WORKS."
- ALFRED THE GREAT

BALDWIN IV OF JERUSALEM

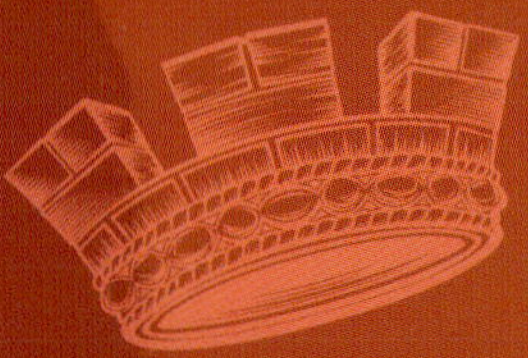

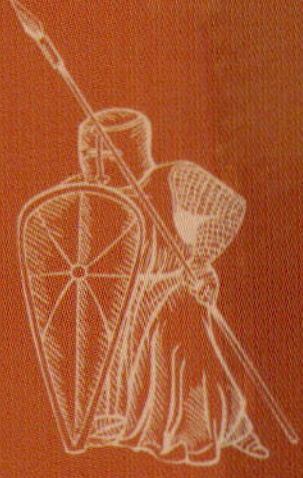

Born: 1161 Died: 1185

Baldwin was born in Jerusalem. His father became king of Jerusalem and Baldwin was next in line to the throne. He began to show signs of a disease called **leprosy** when he was nine years old. Baldwin couldn't feel anything in his right arm, even when somebody pinched him. Although he had the disease, Baldwin was an excellent horse rider and was very clever.

Baldwin became the king of Jerusalem when he was 13 years old. Many people thought that he was too young to be king, but Baldwin was loved by many as he was clever and bold. There were many challenges for the new king. Jerusalem was under attack from a man called Saladin. Saladin led a huge army to attack Jerusalem.

As king, Baldwin couldn't hide from battle. Even though he could only use one arm, Baldwin led his small army to victory against Saladin's bigger army. Although Baldwin won the great battle, he couldn't win against leprosy. He became blind and wanted to stand down as king, but his people loved him and wouldn't let him stand down. Baldwin died when he was 24 and is remembered for his bravery.

BE LIKE BALDWIN IV AND FIGHT ON DESPITE CHALLENGES.

"HE NEVERTHELESS, IN THE SHORT YEARS OF HIS LIFE, DISPLAYED A HEROIC FORTITUDE AND REMARKABLE INTELLIGENCE."

- PROFESSOR MARSHAL W. BALDWIN

QUEEN ELIZABETH I

Born: 1533 Died: 1603

Princess Elizabeth was the second daughter of King Henry VIII, who was the king of England. Although Princess Elizabeth was an **heir** to the throne, her father wanted a son to become king. He had Princess Elizabeth's mother **beheaded** and married another woman, who gave birth to Prince Edward.

Growing up, Princess Elizabeth was very clever. She could speak six languages and play musical instruments. Her half-brother, Prince Edward, became the king of England when he was only nine years old, and her half-sister, Princess Mary, became queen when King Edward died.

Princess Elizabeth became the queen of England when she was 25 years old. A lot of people were unhappy with Queen Mary's rule, so Queen Elizabeth spent a lot of time trying to unite people and make them happy. She tried her to best to avoid fighting in wars, but when faced with war against the Spanish, Queen Elizabeth made sure that the English won.

Queen Elizabeth's rule lasted 44 years. It is known as the Elizabethan Era and is remembered for being a time of growth. Exploration and the arts thrived during her rule – Queen Elizabeth was a fan of the famous **playwright** William Shakespeare and supported English theatres.

"I WILL BE AS GOOD UNTO YE AS EVER A QUEEN WAS UNTO HER PEOPLE."
- QUEEN ELIZABETH I

BE LIKE QUEEN ELIZABETH I AND SUPPORT THE PEOPLE AROUND YOU.

BE LIKE QUEEN ELIZABETH I

ROYAL CROWN

Queen Elizabeth wore a fantastic crown on her head. It had gems all over it. Let's make a crown so that you can be a bold royal like Queen Elizabeth I.

YOU WILL NEED:

- Measuring tape
- Gold card
- Pens and pencils
- Gems
- Stapler
- Scissors
- Glue

MEASURE UP

Before you start making your crown, you'll need to measure your head. Ask an adult to measure around your head in the place where you would like your crown to sit. You'll use this measurement to make your crown.

MAKE IT

1. Cut a strip out of the gold card. Make sure that it is around five centimetres longer than your head measurement and that it is about fifteen centimetres high.

2. Draw triangles along the top of the strip of card.

3. Cut out the triangles to make spikes on the crown.

4. Take the gems and glue them on however you like. You can decorate your crown with drawings if you would like to.

5. When everything is dry, ask an adult to staple the ends of the strip together to form the crown.

6. Wear your crown and rule the world!

Ask an adult to help you.

Will your crown be super shiny and covered in gems?

SITTING BULL

Born: 1831 Died: 1890

Sitting Bull was called Slow as a child because he was slow and careful whenever he did anything. Slow was one of the Hunkpapa people, a Lakota Sioux tribe that was part of the Great Sioux Nation. The Lakota people had lived in America for thousands of years before Europeans arrived in 1492. In 1776, the Europeans founded a country called the US in America.

Slow's father was a warrior called Jumping Bull. Slow fought his first battle when he was 14 years old. He impressed everybody with his bravery and was given the name Sitting Bull.

During this time, Americans from the US began to enter the Sioux Nation. Sitting Bull **defended** the Sioux land against the US Americans. Sitting Bull refused to give up Sioux land or the Sioux way of life. The Sioux people needed to all work together to fight against the US Americans, so Sitting Bull was made the chief of the whole Sioux Nation. He led the Sioux Nation to victory in a great battle, but soon the US Americans forced Sitting Bull and his people to **flee** to Canada.

Sitting Bull and the Sioux people struggled to live in Canada as there was very little food. He made the bold decision to return to America and hand himself in to the US Americans. Whilst in America, Sitting Bull tried his best to keep his way of life. The US Americans feared that Sitting Bull would inspire people to fight against them. This lead to Sitting Bull being shot and killed in 1890.

"LET US PUT OUR MINDS TOGETHER AND SEE WHAT LIFE WE CAN MAKE FOR OUR CHILDREN."

- SITTING BULL

PRINCESS SOPHIA SINGH

Born: 1876 Died: 1948

Princess Sophia Singh was a daughter of Duleep Singh, the last **maharaja** of the **Sikh Empire**. Although her father was Indian, Princess Sophia was born in England because Maharaja Duleep Singh had been exiled when he was 11 years old. Princess Sophia and her six siblings grew up around British royalty – Queen Victoria was her godmother.

Princess Sophia visited India when she was an adult while it was still part of the **British Empire**. She saw many Indians fighting against British rule and saw how many were treated unfairly. This made her eager to fight against **inequality**.

When she returned to England, she joined the **suffragette** movement to fight for women's rights. She became a bold leader within the movement. A lot of people didn't expect a princess to make a bold stand, but Princess Sophia joined 10,000 other women in protest. Some of her protests got her in trouble and she had some belongings taken away by the police when she refused to pay certain **taxes**. Thanks to the actions of Princess Sophia and other suffragettes, in 1918 women over the age of 30 in England were allowed to vote for the first time.

BE LIKE PRINCESS SOPHIA AND HELP PEOPLE WHENEVER YOU ARE ABLE TO.

"WHEN THE WOMEN OF ENGLAND ARE ENFRANCHISED, I SHALL PAY MY TAXES WILLINGLY."

- PRINCESS SOPHIA SINGH

A BOLD TIMELINE

There have been many bold leaders throughout history. Take a look at the timeline to see what empires, tribes and houses the bold people of the past were from.

HATSHEPSUT
BORN 1507 BC
18th Dynasty of Egypt
1540–1295 BC

CYRUS
BORN 590 BC
Persian Empire
550–330 BC

ASHOKA
BORN 304 BC
Mauryan Empire
322–187 BC

CLEOPATRA
BORN 69 BC
Ptolemaic Kingdom
305–30 BC

BOUDICCA
BORN AD 30
Iceni Tribe
220 BC–AD 61

ALFRED
BORN 849
Kingdom of Wessex
519–927

BALDWIN
BORN 1161
Kingdom of Jerusalem
1099–1291

QUEEN ELIZABETH I
BORN 1533
House of Tudor
1485–1603

SITTING BULL
BORN 1831
Great Sioux Nation
Dates uncertain

PRINCESS SOPHIA
BORN 1876
Sikh Empire
1799–1849

GLOSSARY

beheaded	when somebody has had their head chopped off, usually as a punishment
British Empire	an empire that was based in Britain and ruled many countries around the world
Buddhism	a popular religion in Asia which follows the teachings of Buddha
Celtic	relating to the people that lived across central and western Europe
conquered	to have attacked and defeated a place, gaining control of it
cultures	the traditions, ideas and ways of life of groups of people
defended	to have protected something or someone
dharma	teachings in Buddhism
emperor	the ruler of an empire
enfranchised	to have given the right to vote to
First Persian Empire	an empire that ruled parts of where Iran is today
flee	to run away
government	a group of people who make laws in a certain country
heir	someone who will get the objects, money and titles of a person who dies
inequality	when people are not treated fairly or equally
leprosy	a disease that affects the skin and causes loss of feeling in fingers and toes
maharaja	a ruler of an Indian state
Mauryan Empire	an empire that ruled parts of India and other parts of Asia
monks	religious men who usually live together in a monastery
Persia	an area that is where Iran is today
pharaoh	a ruler in ancient Egypt
playwright	a person who writes plays
rebellion	a fight back against the rules of somebody who is in control
regent	somebody who rules in place of a leader who is very young
Roman Empire	an empire that ruled areas across Europe, North Africa and parts of Asia
Sikh Empire	an empire that ruled parts of India
suffragette	a group of women who stood up for women's rights
taxes	money that the government takes from its people to help run the country
trade	buy and sell goods with another place
tribe	a group of people who live in the same area and usually have a shared culture, language or leader
unite	bring together

INDEX